SQUARE

by Robin Nelson

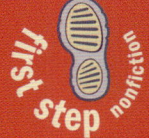

Lerner Publications Company · Minneapolis

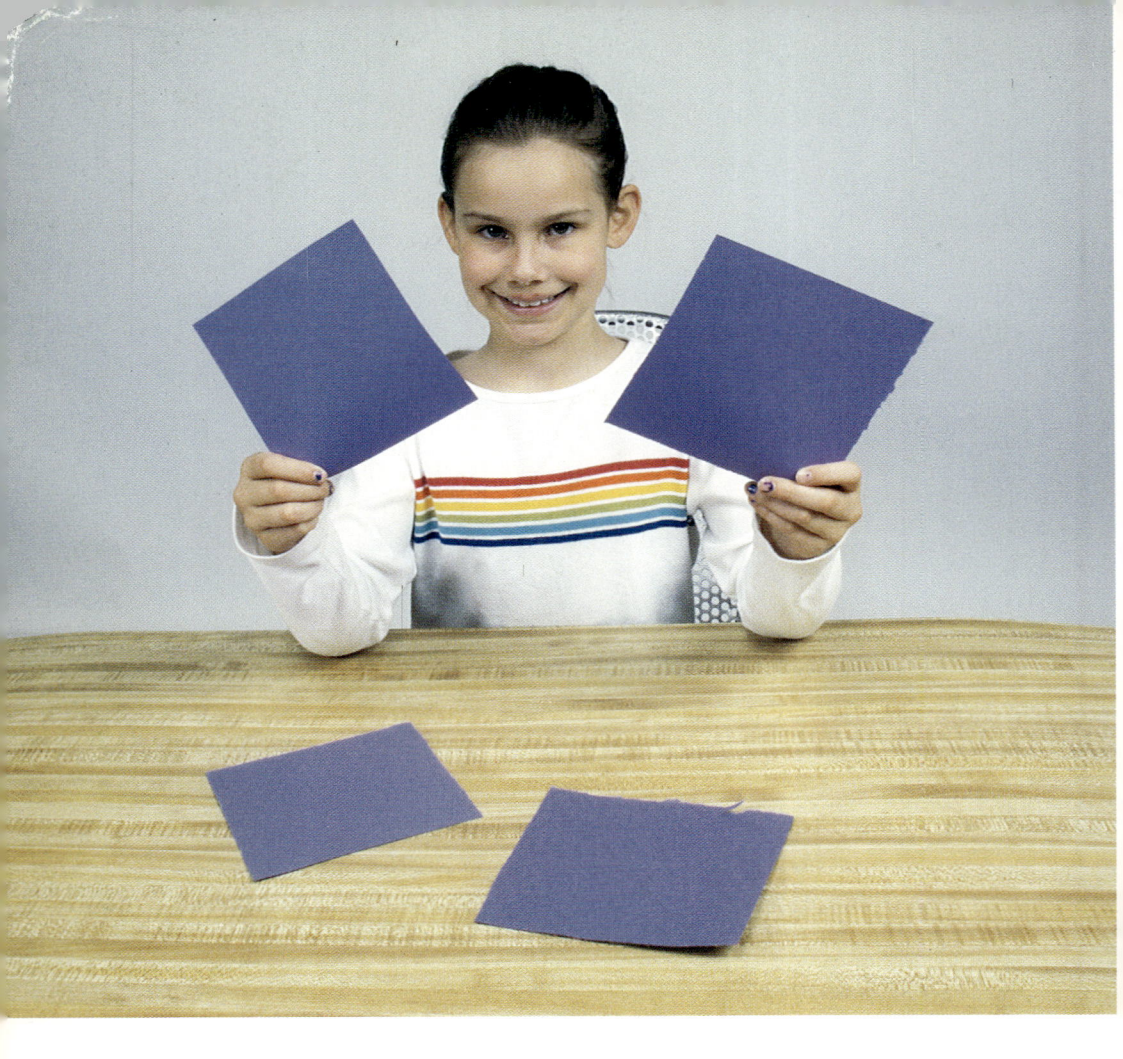

I see squares.

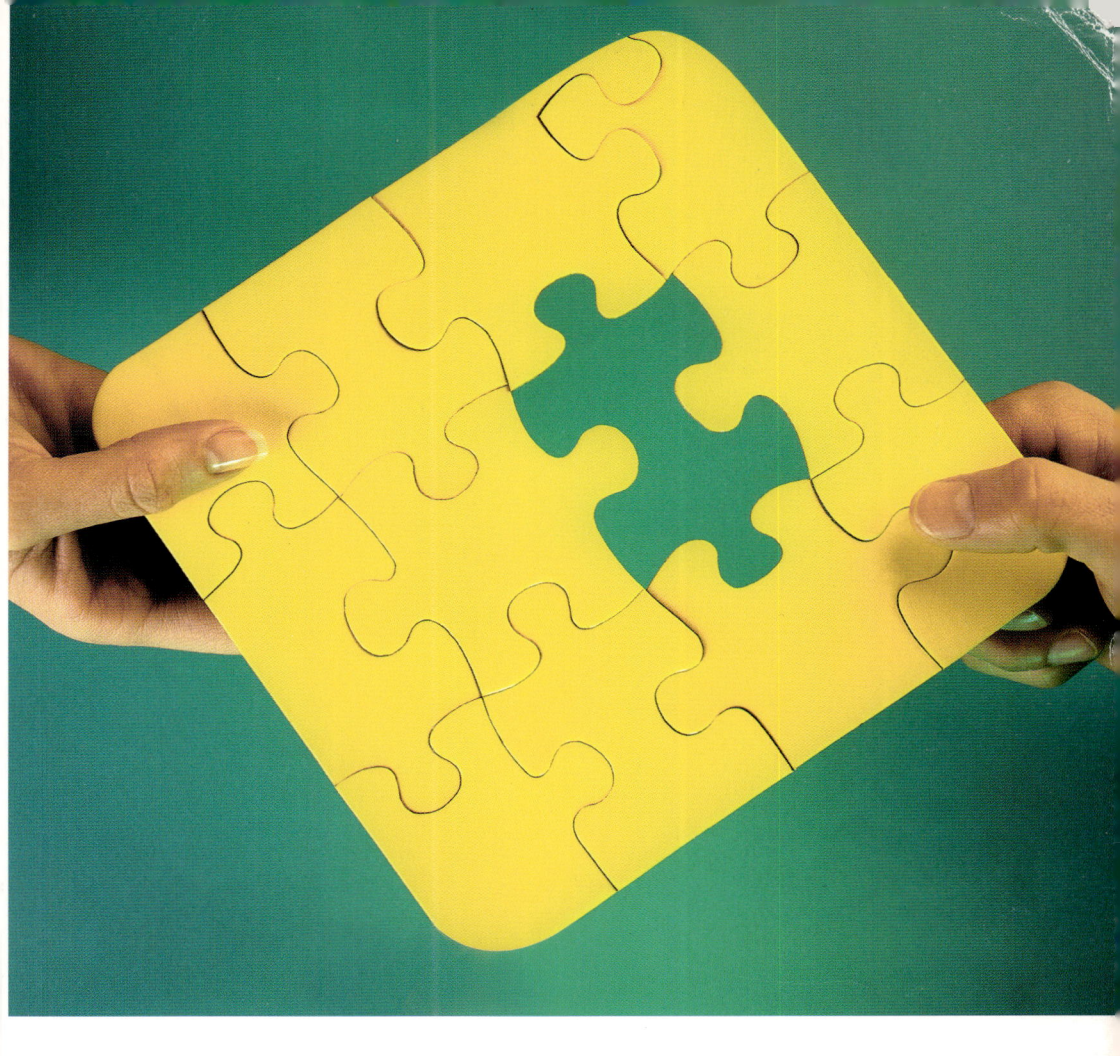

A puzzle is a square.

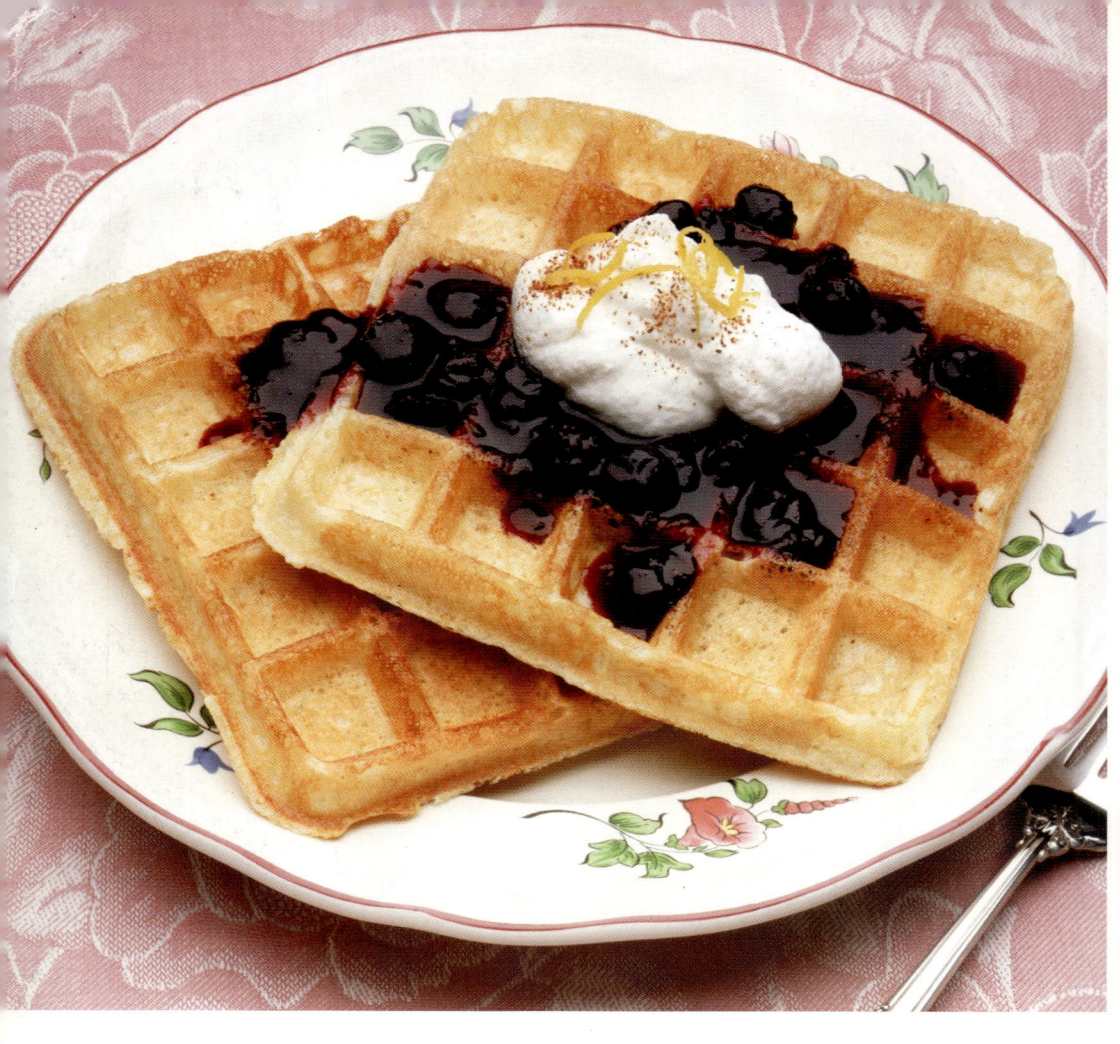

A waffle is a square.

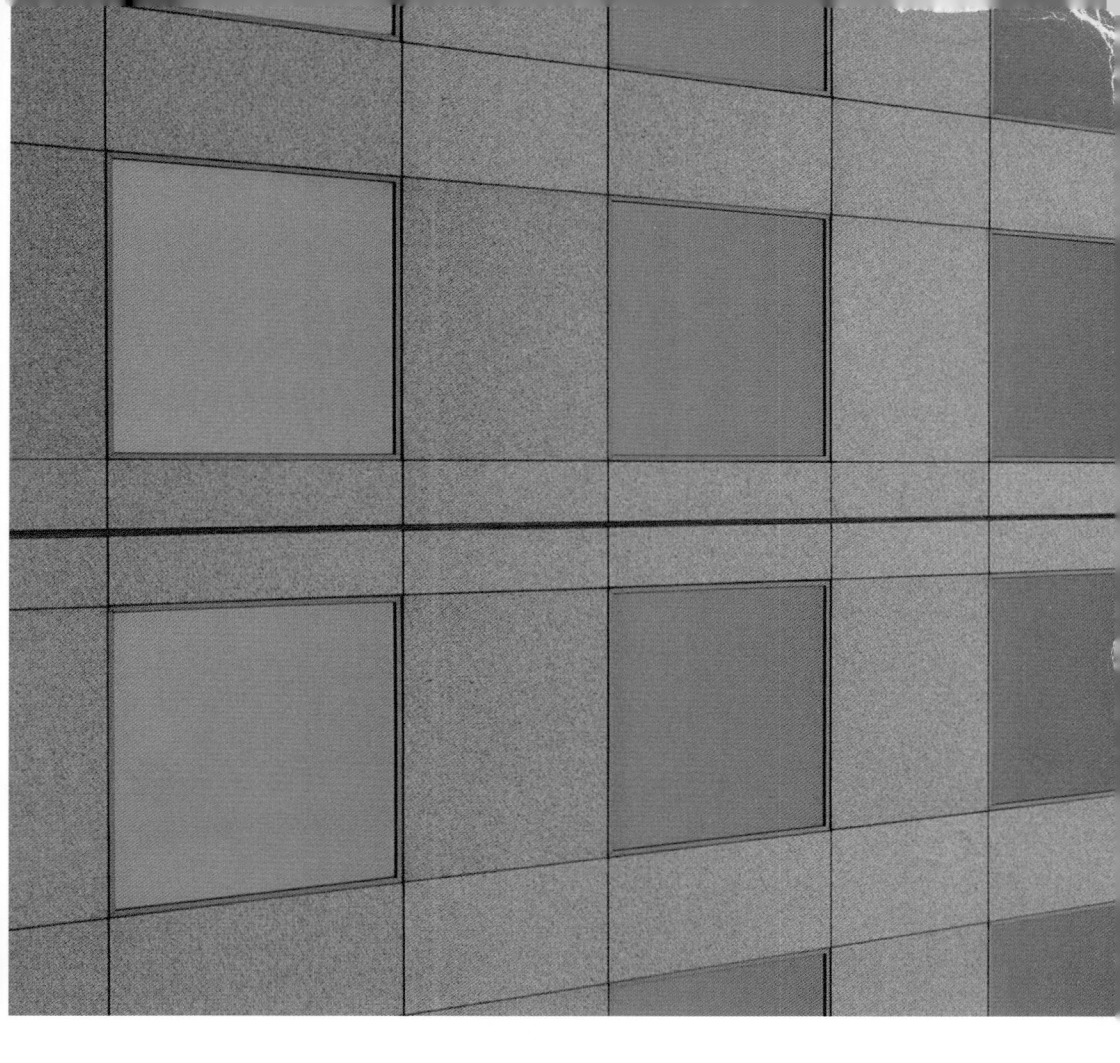

A window is a square.

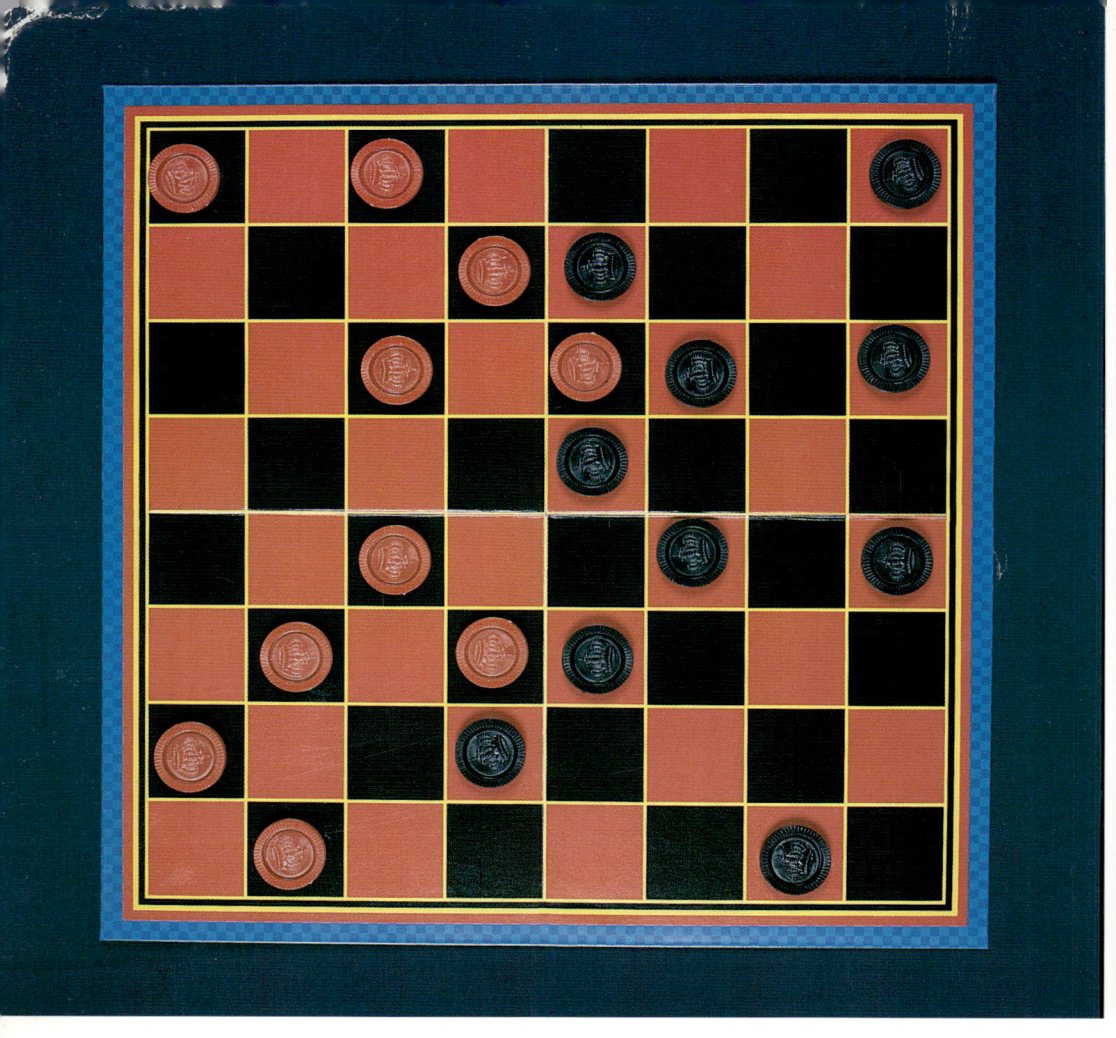

A game is a square.

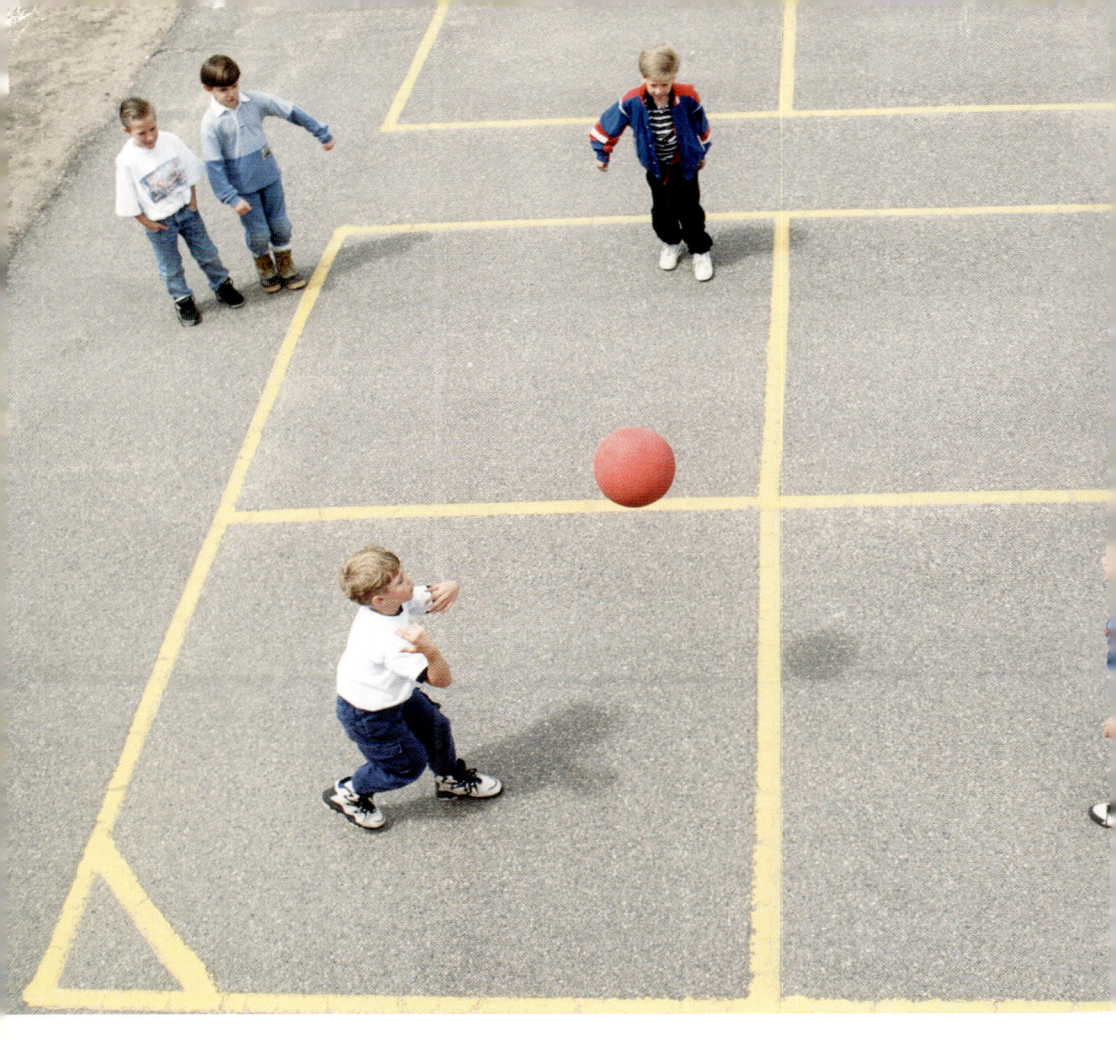

Do you see squares?

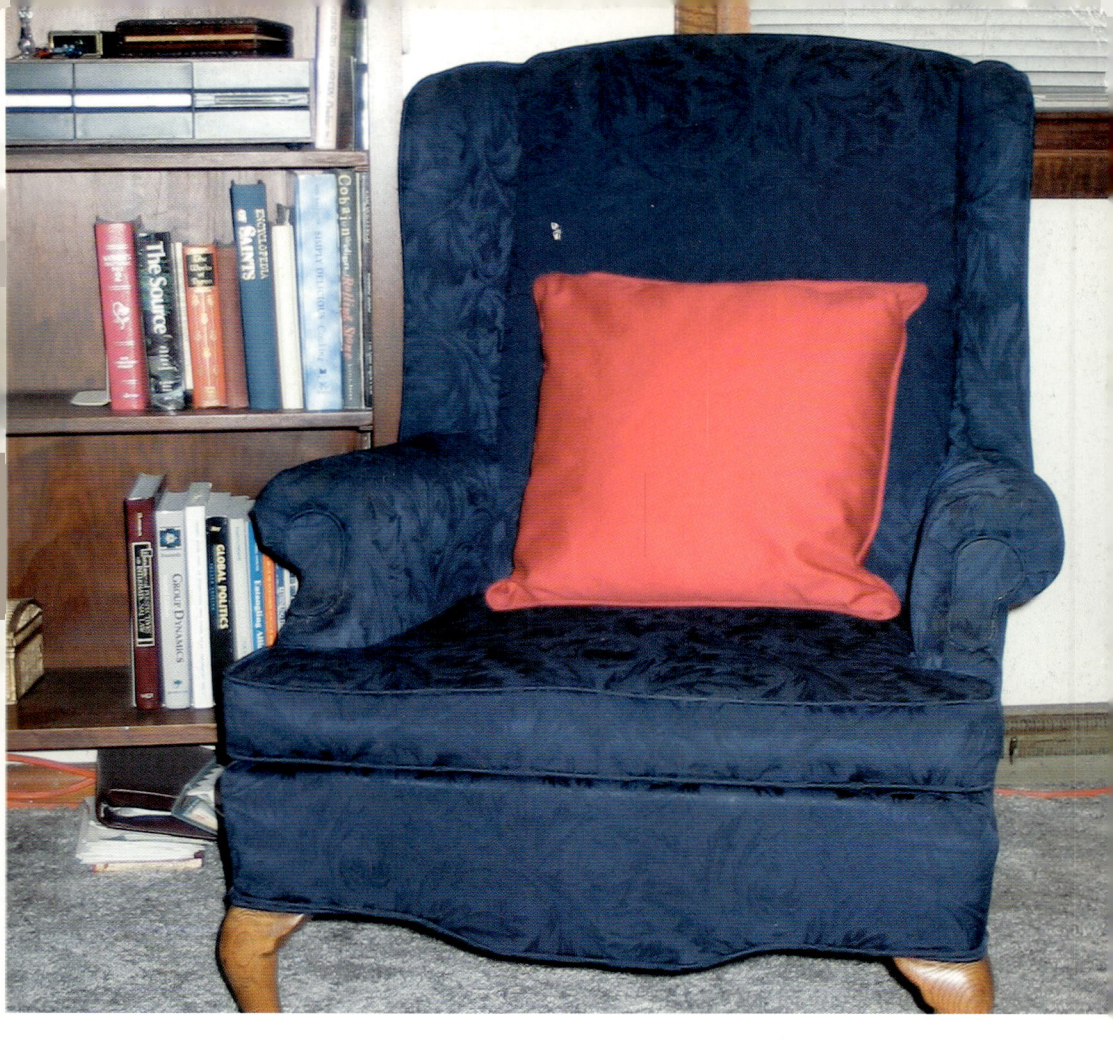

A pillow is a square.